HARCOURT SCHOOL PUBLISHERS
STORYtown

Happy Landings

ISBN 0-15-359604-X

ISBN 978-0-15-359604-9

2 3 4 5 6 7 8 9 10 179 16 15 14 13 12 11 10 09 08 07

Harcourt
SCHOOL PUBLISHERS
www.harcourtschool.com

CONTENTS

Phonics Skill

Read each word. Write the word that names each picture.

1.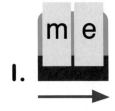

2.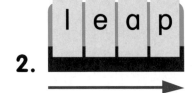

3.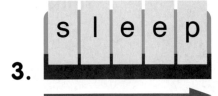

4. _____
   - - - - - - - - - - - - - - - - - - -
   _____

5. _____
   - - - - - - - - - - - - - - - - - - -
   _____

6. _____
   - - - - - - - - - - - - - - - - - - -
   _____

Words to Know

hurry

by

dear

Read each sentence. Circle the word that best completes the sentence.

---

dear   by

I. Rabbit passed _____ Frog.

---

by   dear

2. "You cannot win, _____ Frog!" said Rabbit.

---

hurry   dear

3. Frog wants to win, so he will _____.

Frog and Rabbit

by Sandra Widener

illustrations by Anne Wilson

Frog and Rabbit got set.

"You will see how fast I am," said Rabbit.

"I will beat you."

Frog nodded. "Slow can win, too," he said.

7

Rabbit ran so fast. He passed Frog and kept on going.

Frog kept on leaping. "Slow can win, too," he said.

"Frog can hurry," said Rabbit. "But he will not beat me."

So Rabbit went to sleep.

Frog passed by Rabbit. "Slow can win, too," he said.

Rabbit slept too long. Frog won.
"Dear Rabbit," said Frog. "See?
Slow wins!"

Think Critically

Circle the word or words that best complete each sentence.

race   game

1. Rabbit and Frog ran a _____.

Rabbit   Frog

2. The race was won by _____.

fell asleep   ate a snack

3. Frog finished first because Rabbit _____.

WRITE What do you think Frog did after the race? Write or draw about it.

©Harcourt

13

Phonics Skill

Read each word. Write the word that names each picture.

1.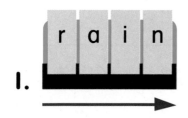

2.

3.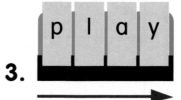

4. _____

5. _____

6. _____

Words to Know

place

dry

warm

cool

Read each sentence. Circle the word that best completes the sentence.

place   cool

1. It rains a lot in a wet _____.

cool   warm

2. The hot sun makes the land _____.

place   cool

3. The wind makes the land _____.

dry   place

4. The land is _____ when it does not rain.

©Harcourt

15

In Each Place

by Pamela Jennett

What can you find in each place?

This place is hot and dry.
It does not rain much.

This place is warm and wet.
It may rain for days.

This place is cold with lots of snow.
In summer, the days are very long.

This place is by the water.
But the land is warm and dry.

This place is by big hills.

It has cool summers and cold winters.

What is it like where you live?

Harcourt

Think Critically

Circle the word or words that best complete each sentence.

coat   swimsuit

1. If you were in a cold place, you would wear a _____.

warm and dry   cold and wet

2. A desert is _____.

sun   rain

3. Some places are dry because there is little _____.

WRITE Write or draw about the weather where you live.

Phonics Skill

Read each word. Write the word that names each picture.

1.

2. l a k e

3. p l a n e

4. _____
   -
   _____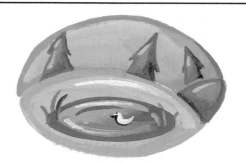

5. _____
   -
   _____

6. _____
   -
   _____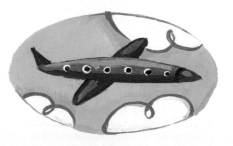

24

Words to Know

oh

open

gone

don't

Read each sentence. Circle the word that best completes the sentence.

---

don't   open

1. The gate is _____!

Gone   Oh

2. _____, no!

---

don't   open

3. I _____ see the cat at all.

---

gone   oh

4. I think the cat is _____.

Max Is Missing!

by Sandra Widener

illustrations by Linda Bronson

In the Play:

Mom

Dad

Dave

Kate

Mom: Oh, no! The gate is open. Max is gone!

Mom: Max! Max! Kate, is the cat
with you?
Kate: No, Mom. I don't see him.

Kate: Max! Max! Dave, is the cat
with you?
Dave: No, Kate, I don't see him.

Dave: Max! Max! Dad, is the cat with you?

Dad: No, Dave. I don't see him.

Mom: How can we get Max back?

Dad: We may have to wait.

Kate: Let's make a path with bits of fish.

Dave: I know! Let's open a can of cat food.

Mom: Max will come back for that!

Kate: Look! Max is back.

Mom: Quick! Go shut the gate!

Think Critically

Circle the words that best
complete each sentence.

little boy   missing cat

1. Max is a _____.

front yard   playground

2. The play takes place in a _____.

open a can   shut the gate

3. The family gets Max back when they _____.

WRITE Write or draw about the part of
the play you like best.

Phonics Skill

Read each word. Write the word that names each picture.

1. 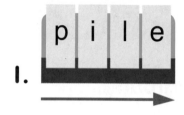 p i l e

2.  n i n e

3.  l i n e

4. _____

5. _____

6. _____

34

Words to Know

right

nice

found

Read each sentence. Circle the word that best completes the sentence.

nice   right

1. It's a _____ day for a picnic!

---

found   right

2. This picnic does not look _____.

---

nice   found

3. We _____ the food!

35

The Picnic Plan

by Sandra Widener

illustrations by Fernando Juarez

What a nice day! Three friends planned
a picnic.

"I like nuts," said Duck. "I will bring a pile of nuts." And she did.

"I like peaches," said Fox. "I will bring a
bunch of peaches." And he did.

"I like apples," said Skunk. "I will bring some ripe apples." And she did.

They went to get dishes and cups. When
they came back, the picnic did not look right.

No nuts. No peaches. No apples. Where
did they go?

"I found them!" said Duck.

"Look who has them!" said Fox.

"Now we will have a picnic," said Skunk.

Think Critically

Circle the word or words that best complete each sentence.

1. The friends plan a picnic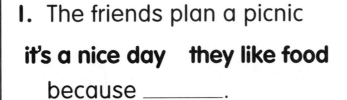

   it's a nice day   they like food

   because _____.

---

   take the food   bring apples

2. It is a problem when the squirrels _____.

   Duck   Fox

3. The missing food is found by _____.

WRITE Write or draw about a time you went on a picnic.

43

©Harcourt

Phonics Skill

Read each word. Write the word that names each picture.

1.  home

2.  hole

3. 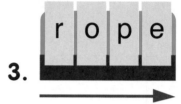 rope

4. _____

5. _____

6. _____

44

©Harcourt

Words to Know

hello

about

would

Mr.

Read each sentence. Circle the word that best completes the sentence.

Mr.   Would

1. _____ Mills meets Cole at the bus stop.

would   hello

2. Cole says _____ to his pals.

about   would

3. Cole _____ like to get on the bus.

about   Mr.

4. Hope tells Cole a joke _____ cats.

©Harcourt

45

School Day

by Sandra Widener

illustrations by Mary Uhles

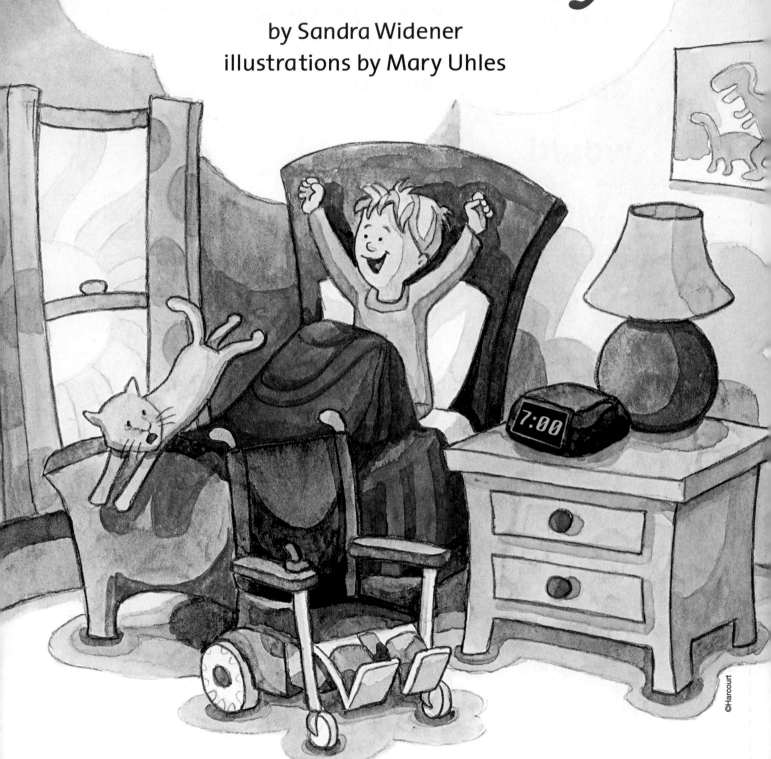

It was time to get up.

Cole got out of bed.

It was time to eat.
Cole had eggs and toast.

It was time to go.

Cole said hello to Mr. Mills.

Then he got on the bus.

It was time for school.
Cole liked math and art.

49

It was time for lunch.
Cole sat next to Hope.
She had good jokes.

It was time to read.

Cole chose a book about bats.

It was time to go home. But that was fine.
Cole would be back at school the next day.

Think Critically

Circle the word or words that best complete each sentence.

bats   art

1. Cole read about _____.

---

told jokes   said hello

2. Cole _____ to Mr. Mills.

---

got up   got on the bus

3. Before Cole ate eggs and toast, he _____.

WRITE What do you like best about your school? Write or draw about it.

Phonics Skill

Read each word. Write the word that names each picture.

1. 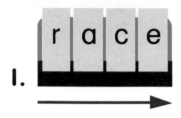 r a c e

2. 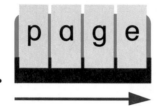 p a g e

3.  b r i d g e

4. _____

5. _____

6. _____

Words to Know

talk

listen

were

four

Read each sentence. Circle the word that best completes the sentence.

were   four

1. Two kids _____ under a bridge.

four   talk

2. The kids start to _____.

Listen   Were

3. "_____!" they said.

four   listen

4. Now, there are _____ kids under the bridge.

©Harcourt

55

Under a Bridge

by Sandra Widener

illustrations by Larry Moore

Two kids were under a bridge.
Grace said, "This bridge can talk. Listen!"

"Hello!" she yelled.
"Hello!" the bridge said back.

57

Four kids were under the bridge.
James said, "This bridge can talk. Listen!"

"Hello!" he yelled.
"Hello!" the bridge said back.

59

Six kids were under the bridge.
Roger said, "I think this bridge can
sing! Listen."

They all started to sing. But someone
sang back. Who was that?

Six kids and a dog were under the bridge.
They all sang. And the bridge sang back.

Think Critically

Circle the word or words that best complete each sentence.

James   the bridge

1. Roger yells hello to _____.

a dog sings back   James sings back

2. The kids are surprised when _____.

3. The kids think the bridge talks back, because

an echo   a rainbow

they hear _____.

WRITE Write or draw about your favorite part of the story.